JOHN THOMPSON'S

FIRST PIANO DUETS

12106

Teachers and Parents

This collection of duets, written in the John Thompson tradition, is intended as supplementary material for the beginning to early elementary level pianist. The pieces may also be used by more advance level students for sight-reading practice. The material is not specifically graded, although pieces appearing later in the book tend to be more demanding than the earlier ones. The first three tunes are for right hand only, and thereafter both hands are employed. Dynamics, phrasing and tempo indications have been deliberately omitted, since initially the student's attention should be focused on playing notes and rhythms accurately. Outline fingering has been included in the student's part, and in general, the hand is assumed to remain in a five-finger position until a new fingering indicates a position shift. The fingering should suit most hands, although logical alternatives are always possible.

THE WILLIS MUSIC COMPANY

Illustrations by xheight Limited

This book copyright © 1996 by Wise Publications
Copyright assigned 1996 to The Willis Music Company

Parts 1+2

Ring-A-Ring O' Roses

Part 1 (Pupil)

Traditional

Little Bird

Part 1 (Pupil)

Traditional

Part 2

Banks of the Ohio

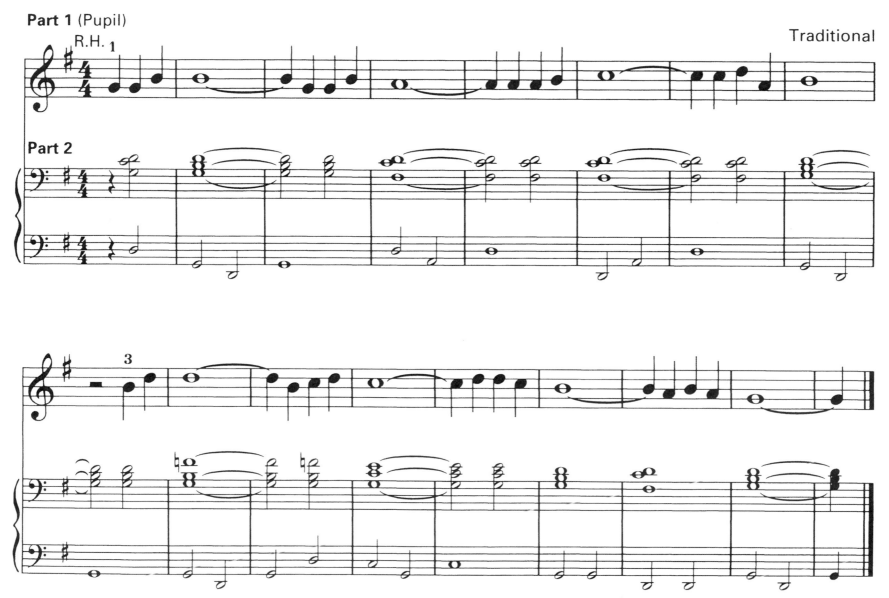

Pussy Cat, Pussy Cat

Traditional

Pussy Cat, Pussy Cat

Traditional

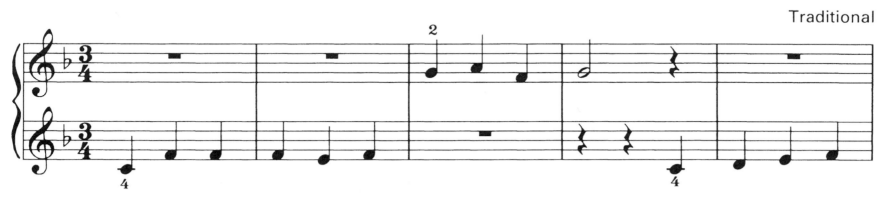

12106

This Old Man

Traditional

Frère Jacques

Traditional

This Old Man

Frère Jacques

Hot Cross Buns

Traditional

Kum Ba Yah

Traditional

Hot Cross Buns

Traditional

Kum Ba Yah

Traditional

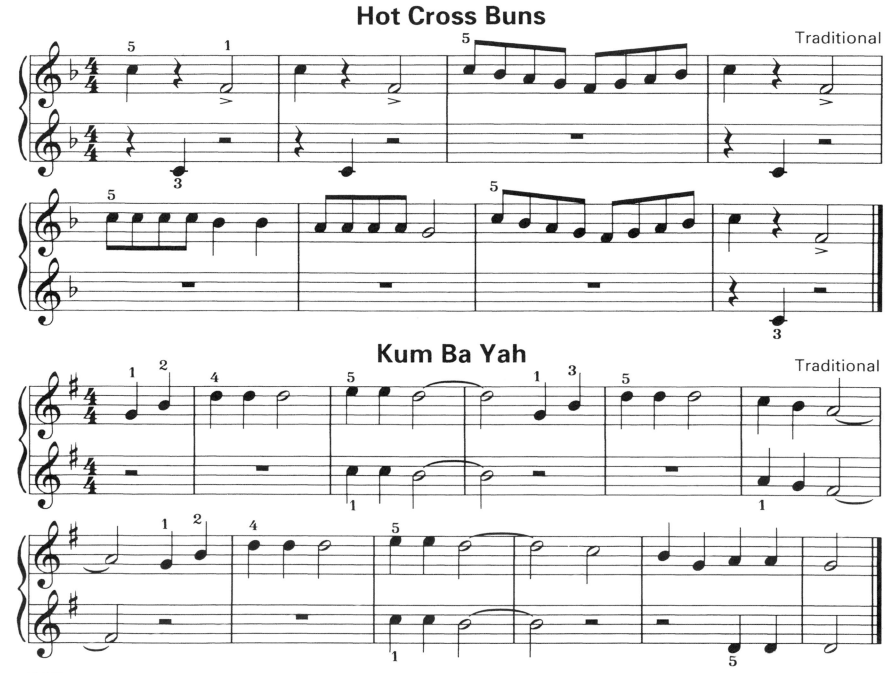

Part 2

We Three Kings

J.H. Hopkins

We Three Kings

J.H. Hopkins

12106

Jingle Bells

J. Pierpont

Jingle Bells

J. Pierpont

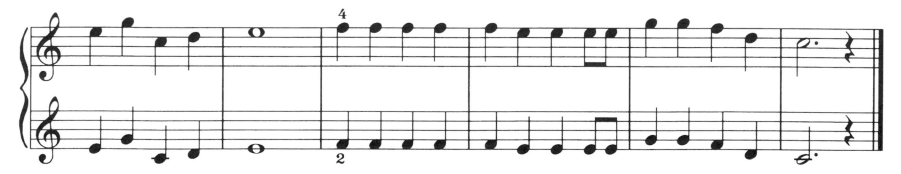

Play either the right hand or the left hand — or even both together!

12106

Land of Hope and Glory

Edward Elgar

Land of Hope and Glory

Edward Elgar

Twinkle, Twinkle, Little Star

Traditional

I Saw Three Ships

Traditional

Twinkle, Twinkle, Little Star

Traditional

Play the notes under the 8va sign an octave higher.

I Saw Three Ships

Traditional

Ode to Joy

Ludwig van Beethoven

Ode to Joy

Ludwig van Beethoven

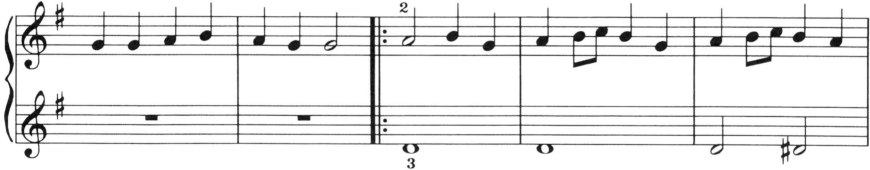

We Wish You a Merry Christmas

Traditional

We Wish You a Merry Christmas

Traditional

Part 2 (Pupil)

The Elephant

Camille Saint-Saëns

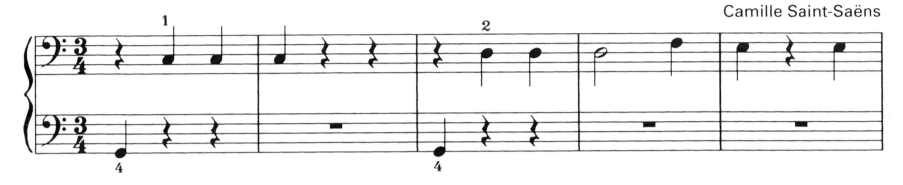

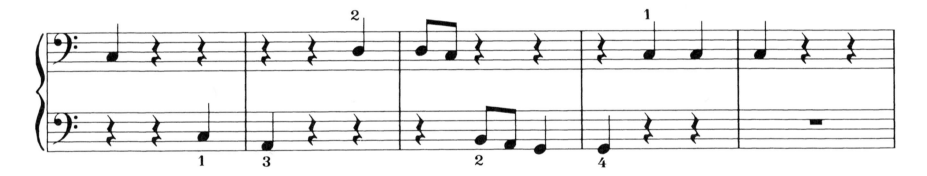

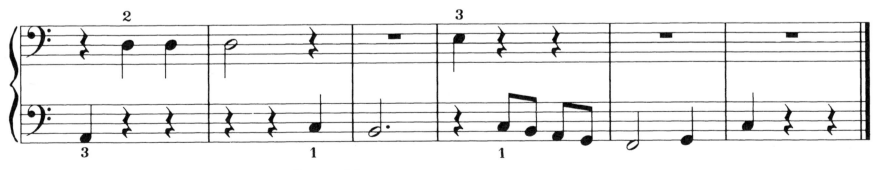

This part may be played an octave lower if you wish.

12106   © 1922 & 1996 Durand S.A. Arranged & Reprinted By Permission Of The Publisher Sole Representative U.S.A. Theodore Presser Company

The Elephant

Camille Saint-Saëns

Country Gardens

Traditional

Country Gardens

Traditional

12106

The Blue Danube

Johann Strauss II

The Blue Danube

Johann Strauss II

The Merry Peasant

Robert Schumann

In this piece the pupil may play either part.

The Merry Peasant

Robert Schumann

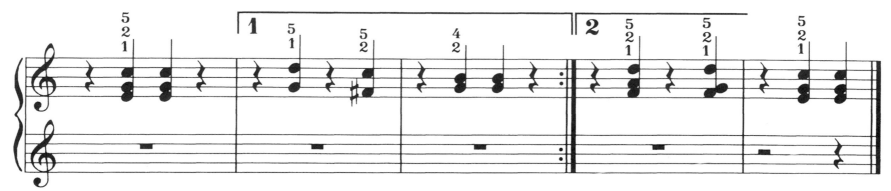

In this piece the pupil may play either part.